For _____

In Memory of _____

From _____

WHEN YOU LOSE SOMEONE YOU LOVE

WRITTEN & ILLUSTRATED BY JOANNE FINK

WHEN YOU LOSE SOMEONE YOU LOVE

CompanionHouse Books™ is an imprint of Fox Chapel Publishers International Ltd.

Vice President–Content: Christopher Reggio

Graphic Design: Angie Vangalis

ISBN 978-1-62008-350-5

Fox Chapel Publishing
903 Square Street
Mount Joy, PA 17552

Fox Chapel Publishers International Ltd.
7 Danefield Road, Selsey (Chichester)
West Sussex PO20 9DA, U.K.

www.facebook.com/companionhousebooks

We are always looking for talented authors. To submit an idea, please send a brief inquiry to acquisitions@foxchapelpublishing.com.

Printed and bound in China
22 21 20 19   2 4 6 8 10 9 7 5 3 1

THIS BOOK IS DEDICATED TO EVERYONE
WHO IS MOURNING THE LOSS
OF SOMEONE THEY LOVE...

Foreword

On August 3rd, my beloved husband, Andy Trattner, lay down to take a nap, had a heart attack while he was sleeping, and never woke up. He was only 53.

When we met at the end of my freshman year of college, his love changed my life; when he died, his loss shattered my world.

For several weeks after Andy died, I was so numb that I wasn't really functional. In fact, if I hadn't had to get up to get our children off to school, I don't think I would have ever gotten out of bed.

I met Andy when I was 18, and we were married for 29 years. He was my husband, my best friend, my business partner, and the father of our two children; his death has profoundly impacted every aspect of my life.

As an artist and writer, I process things by writing and drawing about them. The following pages are from the journal that I started keeping a few weeks after Andy died.

Keeping this journal has been cathartic for me. I am blessed to have incredibly supportive friends and family, and yet it has been hard for me to share with them how alone I feel, how sad I am, and how much I miss Andy. Instead, I've poured my soul into these pages.

I've discovered that grieving is like taking a journey toward an unknown destination against your will: it is incredibly difficult, heartbreaking, and time consuming—and there aren't any shortcuts.

At some point in our lives, most of us will experience the loss of someone we love and will need to deal with that loss in order to move on with our life's journey.

I have been deeply touched when those who have survived their own losses reached out to me with compassion and love. And although I am not very far along on my own journey, I wanted to share my journal in hopes that it will make your grief journey—or the journey of someone you love—a little easier.

Joanne Fink

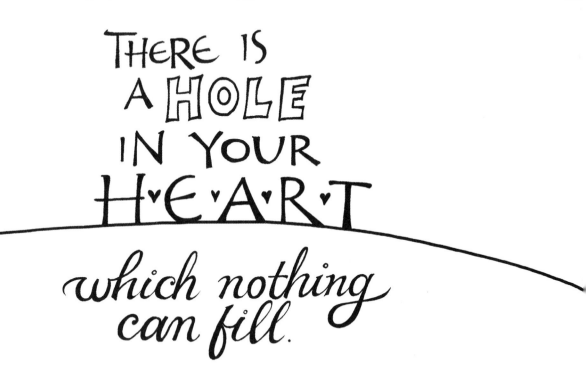

SUDDENLY the WORLD SEEMS UPSIDE DOWN and confusing.

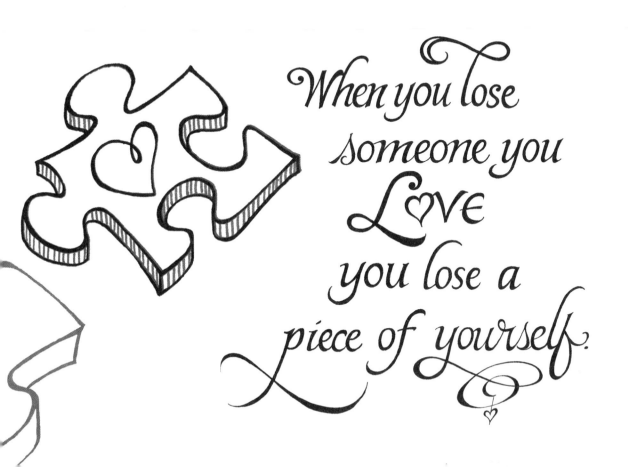

When you lose
someone you
Love
you lose a
piece of yourself.

YOUR LIFE'S JOURNEY VEERS

AND YOU HAVE ABSOLUTELY

When you lose
someone you love

you feel
numb.

some days just surviving is ALL you can do.

WHEN YOU LOSE
SOMEONE YOU LOVE,

it sometimes
seems unfair
that the SUN is still
shining

because a

L·I·G·H·T

in your world

has gone out

and can
never be rekindled.

WHEN YOU LOSE SOMEONE YOU LOVE

EVERYTHING
SEEMS
DISJOINTED

T·I·M·E
seems to move
at a different
p a c e   f o r   y o u
than for everyone else.

Sometimes you are so

WHEN YOU LOSE SOMEONE YOU LOVE...

AND
YOU OFTEN
FEEL AFRAID
AND OVERWHELMED.

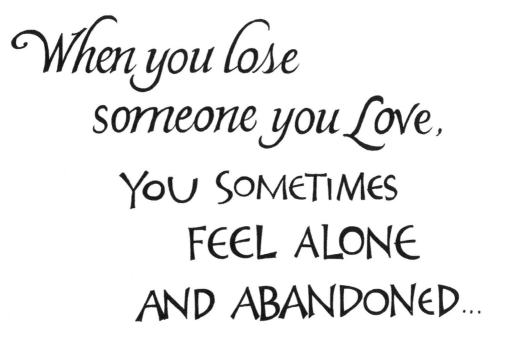

When you lose
someone you Love,
YOU SOMETIMES
FEEL ALONE
AND ABANDONED...

NOT ONLY BY THE PERSON YOU LOST,
BUT BY EVERYONE WHO
EXPRESSES SYMPATHY

AND THEN
GOES ON WITH THEIR LIVES...

WHEN YOUR WORLD WILL

never

BE

THE

SAME

AND YOUR *Heart breaks* WHEN YOU REALIZE

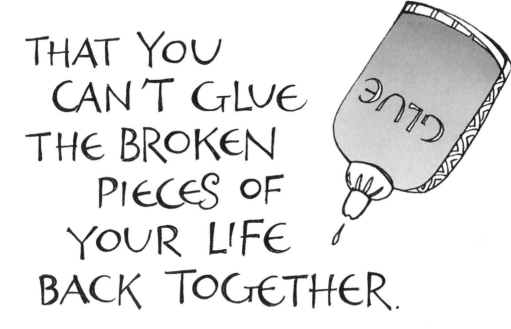

THAT YOU
CAN'T GLUE
THE BROKEN
PIECES OF
YOUR LIFE
BACK TOGETHER.

When you lose someone you love
you sometimes get
REALLY ANGRY
with them for not
being here with you...

and then you get

REALLY ANGRY
WITH YOURSELF

for feeling that way.

WHEN YOU LOSE
SOMEONE YOU LOVE...

YOU BECOME MORE FEARFUL
BECAUSE YOU REALIZE

THERE ARE NO GUARANTEES IN LIFE

AND YOU WORRY ABOUT LOSING OTHER PEOPLE YOU LOVE

When you lose someone you Love,

IT TAKES A LONG TIME
BEFORE YOU STOP
PICKING UP THE PHONE
TO CALL THEM.

AND YOU'D GIVE ALMOST

Anything

IF YOU COULD JUST SEE THEM
ONE MORE TIME...

THERE ARE DAYS
YOU WONDER

HOW YOU CAN
GO ON WITHOUT THEM...

SOME DAYS
you don't want to

OTHER DAYS
YOU WANT TO
Live your best life
TO MAKE THEM
PROUD OF YOU.

When you lose
someone
you Love,

YOU CAN BE OK
FOR HOURS OR
EVEN DAYS AT A TIME
and then totally lose it
for NO reason at all

OR MORE LIKELY
YOU PROBABLY LOST IT
BECAUSE YOU SAW
OR DID SOMETHING

YOU WANTED TO SHARE
WITH YOUR LOVED ONE
AND REALIZED (AGAIN) THAT
they aren't there...

... AND THAT THEY AREN'T *EVER* COMING BACK.

MOST PEOPLE DON'T FULLY APPRECIATE

THE *Miracle* OF *life*

UNTIL THEY HELP BRING
A BABY INTO THE WORLD

AND MOST PEOPLE DON'T LEARN THAT

Love is Eternal

UNTIL THEY LOSE SOMEONE
THEY CHERISH AND REALIZE THAT ...

You don't stop loving someone just because they aren't here anymore.

& THE Legacy YOU WANT TO LEAVE

INK

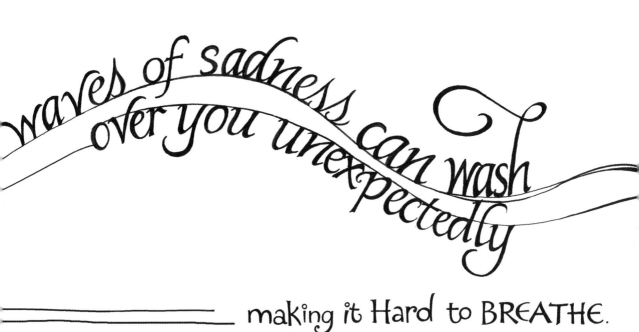

waves of sadness over you unexpectedly can wash

making it Hard to BREATHE.

IT IS HARD TO SLEEP...
EVEN WEEKS AND
MONTHS LATER

WHEN YOU LOSE SOMEONE YOU LOVE YOU HAVE TO rediscover yourself.

THE SEARCH FOR MEANING

Who am I?

Where am I headed?

What do I need to grow?

How can I become who I am supposed to be?

There
are days
you put a
mask on

and pretend
everything is "OK"
when someone asks
how you are...

WHEN YOU LOSE SOMEONE YOU LOVE
it is HARD *to go places*
ESPECIALLY PARTIES
AND CELEBRATIONS
without them.

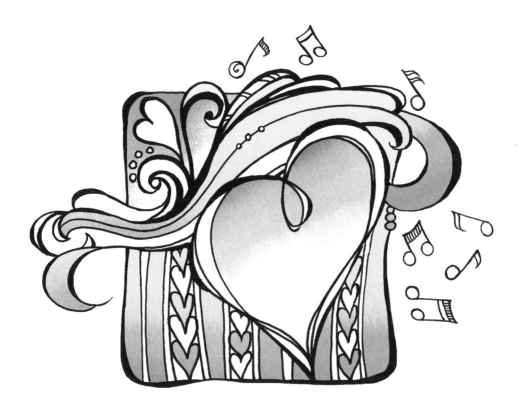

You miss a lot of things about them...
but you miss their hugs,
and hearing them laugh,
most of all

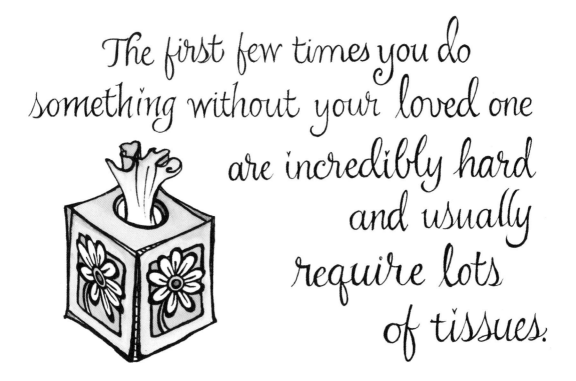

The first few times you do something without your loved one are incredibly hard and usually require lots of tissues.

When
You
Lose
Someone
You
Love

YOU DISCOVER
   WHO YOUR TRUE
      FRIENDS ARE...

   AND HOW VERY
IMPORTANT FAMILY
 & FRIENDS CAN BE.

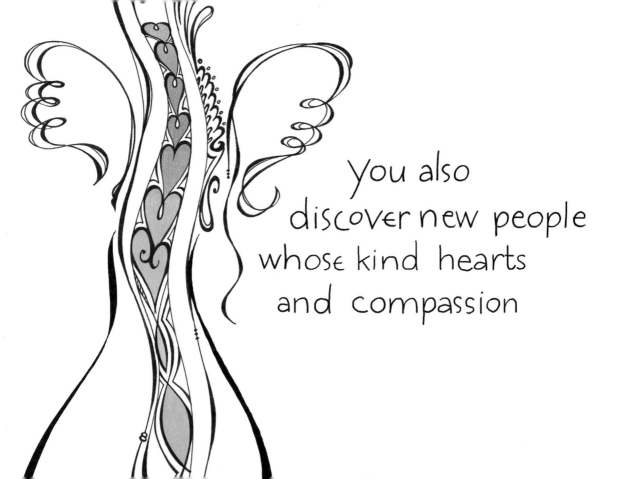

You also
discover new people
whose kind hearts
and compassion

touch you
in ways you would never
have dreamed before your
loved one died.

When you lose someone you love
you appreciate photos of them
more than you ever
dreamed possible...

and you wish you had a recording
of their voice saying "I love you"
so you could listen to it
whenever you want.

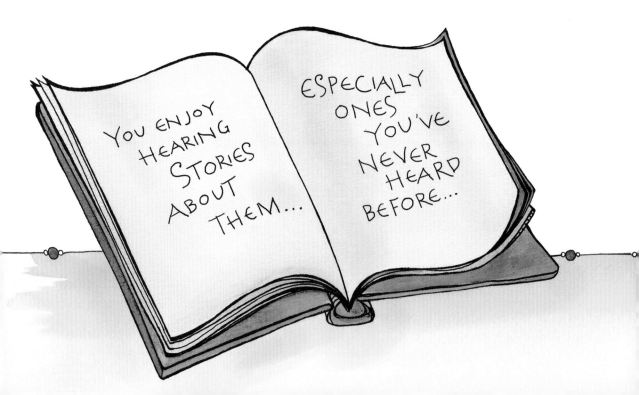

IT CAN HELP TO REMINISCE
WITH FRIENDS & FAMILY
WHO SHARE YOUR LOSS

WHEN YOU LOSE SOMEONE YOU LOVE

YOU BEGIN
YOUR LIFE'S
JOURNEY ANEW...

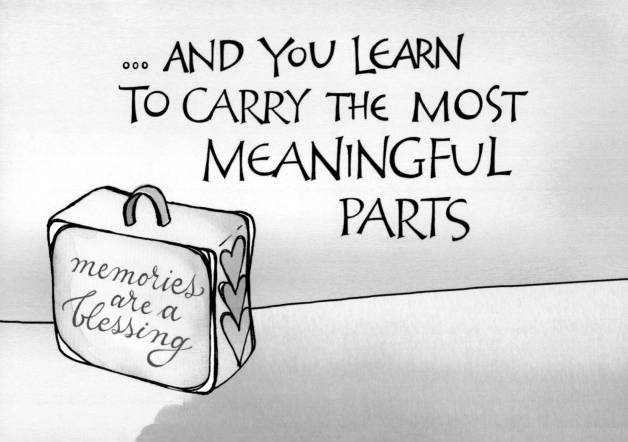

OF YOUR OLD LIFE
WITH YOU ON
YOUR JOURNEY

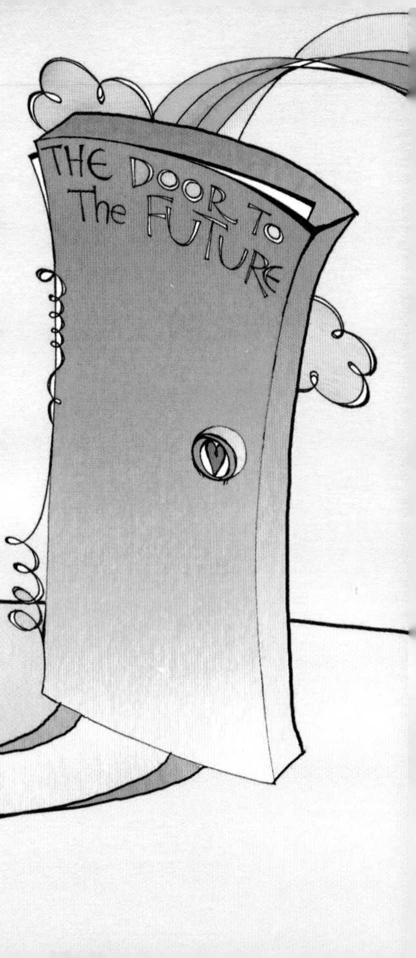

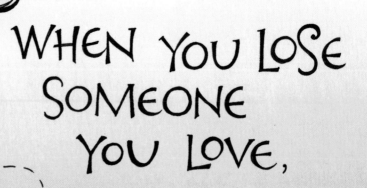

WHEN YOU LOSE
SOMEONE
YOU LOVE,

Everything CHANGES

Even the things you wish would remain the same.

You remember all
the things which
make them so special...

and you look for ways
to keep their memory
vibrantly, alive.

WHEN YOU LOSE SOMEONE YOU LOVE,

YOU LEARN THAT
YOU CAN SURVIVE THE
UNIMAGINABLE...

ONE **DAY** AT A TIME

ONE **STEP** AT A TIME

ONE **BREATH** AT A TIME

ONE **PRAYER** AT A TIME

WHEN YOU LOSE SOMEONE YOU LOVE
IT HELPS TO LOOK
UP AT THE STARS
AND IMAGINE
THAT THE LIGHT OF
YOUR LOVED ONE'S S·O·U·L

IS
SHINING
DOWN UPON
Y·O·U
TO LIGHT YOUR WAY

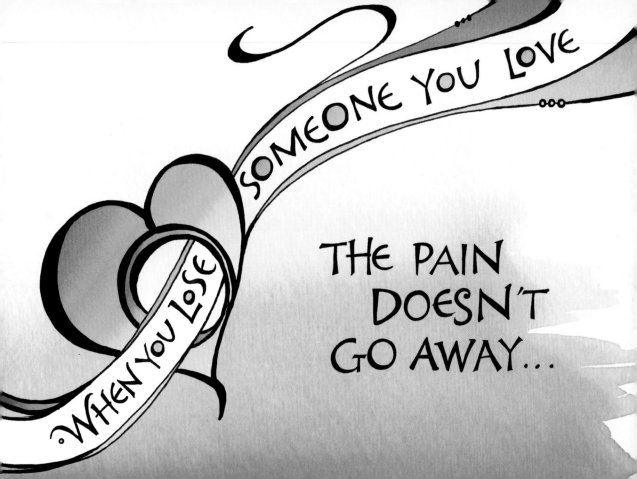

IT DOES GET
EASIER TO BEAR

WHEN YOU LOSE
SOMEONE YOU LOVE

Epilogue

It has been six years since I wrote the first draft of this book. Although there are still days I feel profoundly dysfunctional, fortunately those days occur less frequently. I think this is true for our children, too; they both occasionally have bad days, but we have all regained some equilibrium and a sense of purpose. Special thanks to my coloring book publisher, Fox Chapel Publishing, for publishing this edition of *When You Lose Someone You Love*. This allows me to focus on my new goal: changing the culture of grief support in America.

Recently, I launched *WhenYouLoseSomeone.com*, a website with resources both for those who have lost loved ones and for those who are supporting people dealing with loss. If this book touched your heart, you may be interested in reading my biweekly blog, *The Journey from Grief to Gratitude*, which includes illustrations from my journals, stories about my grief journey, as well as some of my commemorative art. I hope that sharing what I've learned on my own grief journey will help you on yours.

Andy was an awesome dad, and nothing was more important to him than our children. I marvel as they continue to grow into grounded, caring individuals, and I take joy in knowing how very proud their father would be of them. Our son inherited some of Andy's best qualities: intelligence, stage presence, humor, and a deep sense of integrity. Our daughter continually strives to become the person she knows her dad wants her to be. While I process things by putting pen to paper, Samantha processes her grief musically. It took her three years to write the song "Legacy," an amazing tribute to her dad. My favorite lyrics are:

You're everything I see; not just a memory...
You'll live on through me; I am your legacy.

When you lose someone you love, you often feel lost and alone and aren't sure how to get your life back on track. If you have recently lost someone you love, please know that there is no time frame for grief. Everyone grieves at their own pace and in their own way; each person's grief journey is different. There is a chasm that separates those who have experienced profound loss from those who haven't, and once you've crossed it, you're forever changed—but you are not alone. It really helps to be with people who have also experienced loss and can understand, at least on some level, what you are going through, and I encourage you to find a grief support group in your area or online.

If you would like to connect with others who have lost someone they love, there are helpful resources on the *WhenYouLoseSomeone.com* website and the "When You Lose Someone You Love" Facebook page. Andy was committed to making a difference in the world. I celebrate his life and honor his memory by sharing stories about him, supporting things I know he valued, and mentoring others who are grieving. There has not been a single day when I have not thought about him; his light lives on in my heart.

Andy's death has taught me so much about life—I have grown in ways that I never would have imagined before he died. I know I am a more compassionate and caring person today because I understand firsthand how devastating it is to lose someone you love.

With sympathy for your loss,

Joanne Fink

Please connect with me at
WhenYouLoseSomeone.com and be
sure and check out my blog,
The Journey from Grief to Gratitude.

Love
is
Eternal

Additional copies of

WHEN YOU LOSE
SOMEONE YOU LOVE

available through
www.FoxChapelPublishing.com
www.WhenYouLoseSomeone.com